Teach Your Cat
TRICKS

Cover images from Shutterstock.com

Interior images from Shutterstock.com except p. 22, 24–32, 46 by Christopher Hiltz

Contributing writer: Donald Vaughan

Louis Weber, CEO
Publications International, Ltd.
8140 Lehigh Avenue
Morton Grove, Illinois 60053

Permission is never granted for commercial purposes.

ISBN: 978-1-68022-019-3

Manufactured in China.

8 7 6 5 4 3 2 1

Table of Contents

Welcome to cat OWNERSHIP

> Take us home and your life will never be the same again!

Whether you're playing with an active kitten or snuggling with a beloved older cat, having a cat is one of life's greatest pleasures. This book is designed to help you enhance that experience.

In the first section, we'll talk about some basic, easy ways to make your cat comfortable in your home—and to protect your own belongings. The second section, on play, will help you keep your cat healthy, happy, and frustration-free. You'll find instructions for making your own cat toys, including the feathered cat training toy contained in this kit. In the final section of this book, you'll find easy, clear instructions for training your cat.

To some people, the idea of teaching a cat tricks is a ridiculous one. They believe that only a rare cat will agree to it. But while cats are independent, they can learn and enjoy doing tricks such as shaking hands, eating on cue, and running an obstacle course. We'll give you plenty of helpful hints on making the training effective and enjoyable for your pet.

Whether your pet is one you've had for years or one you just recently made a home for, you'll find useful information in these pages for keeping kitty occupied and content.

Being a cat caretaker is easy. Let me walk you through the steps!

Sharing a home with YOUR CAT

Happy is the home with at least one cat.

—Italian proverb

THE BASIC NECESSITIES

Litter boxes and litter should be the first things you buy when you decide to get a cat. Get them set up before the cat sets even a single paw in your house. Make sure the litter boxes are clean, easy to find, and numerous enough.

> Don't place our litter box near the food bowl. Would you want to eat in your bathroom?

THINK LIKE YOUR CAT

As you're setting up litter boxes for your cat, try to put yourself in your cat's place. Crouch or kneel down and look around. What do you see? What can you smell? An enclosed space, where the cat can't see what might be coming his way, can make your cat feel unsafe. Enclosed spaces may trap smells, too; remember that your cat's sense of smell is more acute than yours!

EASY TO FIND

If your home has more than one floor, put a litter box on each floor. Particularly as cats get older, they may not be able to make a trek up or down stairs very quickly.

A li'l privacy, please!

HOW MANY?

Many cats dislike using a box that has been used recently (even if it was used by that very cat herself), so the rule of thumb is: the number of litter boxes in the house should equal the number of cats in the house plus one.

KEEP YOUR CAT IN HIS PLACE

Has your cat chosen a new location in your home for an "invisible" litter box? Squirt some lemon juice on a cotton ball, put it in a lidded tea strainer, and hang it over the fragrant location. Kitty should be repelled by the smell and seek out the real litter box.

STOP THE CAT FROM "WATERING" THE GARDEN

To keep your cat from using the garden as her personal litter box, mix orange peels with dried, used coffee grounds and sprinkle the mixture around the plants. That will keep her away.

WANTED

CRIMES AGAINST BOTANY
GARDEN-VARIETY OFFENSES

READING YOUR CAT

A telltale clue to a cat's mood is the position of her tail. A mere flick of the tail can relay a message worth a thousand words.

A vertical tail indicates a friendly welcome.

An upright tail bent forward displays dominance.

A wagging tail can signal ambivalence, anger, or annoyance.

When the tail curves down and up, kitty is calm and content.

SCRATCHING POSTS

You love your cat, but you don't love clawed furniture. What can you do?

Every kind of cat—from lions and cheetahs to Siamese and alley cats—has an instinctive need to scratch. Scratching behavior serves three functions:

 marking territory

 keeping the cat's claws in proper condition

 stretching the muscles and ligaments in the toes and feet

Not even declawing will stop this behavior. Since you can't stop the scratching, you'll need to make sure you can limit it to the places you choose. A good scratching post can accomplish just that.

Blueprint of a good
SCRATCHING POST

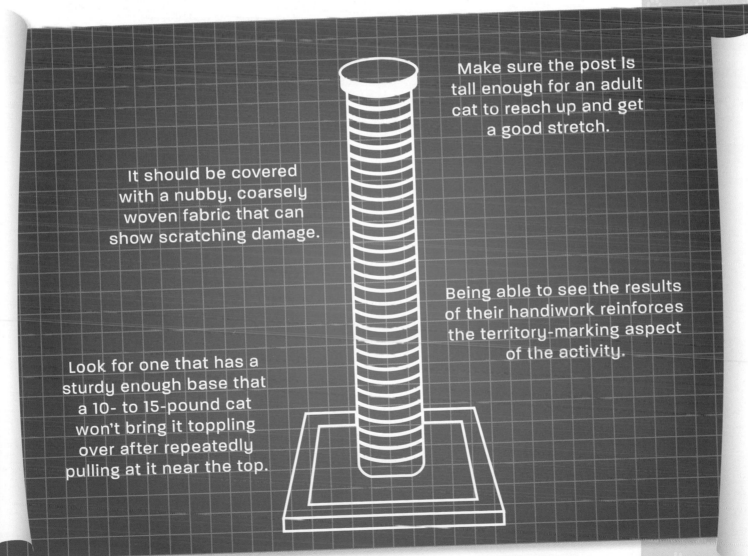

Make sure the post Is tall enough for an adult cat to reach up and get a good stretch.

It should be covered with a nubby, coarsely woven fabric that can show scratching damage.

Being able to see the results of their handiwork reinforces the territory-marking aspect of the activity.

Look for one that has a sturdy enough base that a 10- to 15-pound cat won't bring it toppling over after repeatedly pulling at it near the top.

Bleh!

PROTECT YOUR HOUSEPLANTS

Keep your cat from digging in the soil of a houseplant. Get a plastic mesh produce bag or mesh wine-bottle sleeve big enough to cover the surface of the dirt. Cut a slit in the mesh to fit the size of the plant; place this "collar" over the dirt.

A MORE AROMATIC ALTERNATIVE

Push two or three cinnamon sticks into the soil in each potted houseplant that seems to interest your dog or cat. Smells nice, doesn't it? Not to your pet!

I told Claude he was in for a bit of a shock if he continued to chew on the electrical cords! He never listens.

KEEP YOUR CAT CLEAR OF POWER CORDS

If your pet likes to gnaw on electrical cords, wipe the cords with liquid hand cleanser. One taste, and he won't be back for more.

Holy cat tree! Check out Fluffy— she's living the dream!

CLIMBING CATS

Cats are natural vertical climbers and leapers. In other words, the higher a cat can go, the happier he often is. It's no big deal for a young, healthy cat to make a straight jump from the floor to a flat surface four or five feet off the ground.

To keep your cat from climbing in places he shouldn't, you can build or buy one or more cat trees—a central post with perches and enclosed hiding places. Use a large tree limb as the central post to give the piece a more natural look and make it more inviting for the cat.

The base must be wide, sturdy, and well-weighted to prevent tipping over. The perches and hidey-holes can be carpeted to make them more comfortable and help blend in with your decor or color schemes.

Half the time I'm not exactly sure how I got up here either.

Playing with
YOUR CAT

When I play with my cat,
who knows if I am not a pastime
to her more than she is to me?

—Michel de Montaigne

IT'S TIME TO PLAY!

Playing with your cat is a win-win situation: It's fun for both of you, it's good for your cat's physical and mental well-being, and there's nothing cuter than a playing cat. Here are some tips so you and your cat can get the most of playtime.

 Provide your cat with a variety of toys. Rotate out toys so she doesn't get bored.

🐾 When you're playing with a toy that mimics hunting, such as the feathered cat training toy included in this kit (see page 24), make sure make sure your cat succeeds in catching the "prey" before you put the toy away. A successful "hunt" will make your cat happy and pleased to play again.

🐾 Playing before mealtime is a natural fit for cats. You can also incorporate food into the play session to satisfy your cat's instincts. Hide a food treat in a bottle with a large mouth and let your cat get it out, or hide tidbits around the room and let your cat go on a treasure hunt.

🐾 Hide a feather or cotton mouse underneath pillows, a T-shirt, or a loose pile of newspapers. Cats love hidden prey.

GOTCHA!

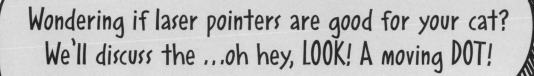

Wondering if laser pointers are good for your cat? We'll discuss the ...oh hey, LOOK! A moving DOT!

LASER POINTERS

Letting your cat chase the dot from a laser pointer is an inexpensive, fun, entertaining way to give your cat some exercise. If you add this toy to your repertoire, though, keep a few things in mind for maximum safety and enjoyment:

- 🐾 Never shine the light in your cat's eyes. Make sure to put away the toy in a place where your cat can't find it and accidentally turn it on.

- 🐾 Cats love chasing prey, but ultimately they love catching it most. Some cats find a laser pointer dot frustrating because they can't physically catch it. If your cat seems to get wound up or frustrated, this may not be the toy for him.

- 🐾 Keep play sessions short. Throughout the session, rest the dot on something your cat can pounce on, another toy or a bit of food. This helps satisfy your cat's need to finish the hunt.

A PLAYTIME DON'T

Never allow or encourage a new kitten or cat to play with your bare hand or foot. A tiny kitten may look cute batting at your thumb, but you'll be singing a different tune when she repeats those behaviors as a full-grown cat.

If your cat tries to pounce on, bite, or otherwise capture and conquer your hand or foot, withdraw and say "no" calmly but firmly. Provide other toys that will let your cat fulfill that instinct, such as the cat training toy included in this kit (see page 24). However, take care not to give the substitute toy right as the kitten is pouncing on you—that just teaches them that a bad behavior will get a treat!

AROUND THE HOUSE

You don't need to spend a lot of money on toys for your cat. In fact, your cats will probably have just as much fun playing with these common household objects!

Corks and milk rings

Milk rings should be the hard plastic variety that kitty can't easily chew and digest.

Bubbles

Make sure to purchase the nontoxic variety.

A crumpled ball of paper

A brown paper bag

To keep kitty safe,
remove any handles in
which they may get caught.

Put a ping-pong ball
or another small treat
in an old tissue box
and watch us try
to get it out!

Shower curtain rings

Some household objects should not be used as toys, as they're danger-ous for the cat. Avoid plastic bags, rubber bands, paper clips, and string. Toys—homemade or purchased—that have elements that could be swal-lowed should only be played with under supervision.

FISHING POLE TOY

What you'll need:

Pieces included in kit

Nontoxic glue (optional)

Pole toys are great for letting your cat hunt. As you play, mimic prey that starts and stops, moving backward and sideways. Your cat will be motivated to catch the toy, so use it as a training tool to distract your cat from other objects (see page 21), to focus your cat's attention to an area (see page 56), or to lure your cat where you want her to go (see pages 60 and 62).

Caution: Because this toy has small parts, kitty should only play with it under your supervision.

Step 1

Gather together the feathers, arranging the longer yellow feathers in the center.

Step 2

Wrap one end of the cord around the end of the feathers and fasten it securely. You may want to use glue.

Step 3

Slide the long plastic piece over the end of the cord.

Step 4

Secure the piece tightly over the end of the feathers. Glue may help to keep the piece in place.

Step 5

Place the other end of the cord at the end of the long plastic tube. Secure it with one of the plastic caps. Place the other plastic cap on the other end of the tube.

On a Roll
RATTLE

What you'll need:

An empty toilet paper roll

A treat

I was helping.

Step 1

Fold down one end of the roll.

Step 2

Place the treat inside.

Step 3

Fold down the other end of the roll.

Step 1

Glue the green cloth around the rolls.

Step 2

Feed the string or ribbon through each toilet paper roll.

Step 3

Glue the string to the inside of the roll.

On a Roll
SNAKE

What you'll need:

Three or more empty toilet paper rolls or paper towel rolls

A long string or ribbon

Nontoxic glue

Green cloth

EENY MEENIE MINIE MOUSE

What you'll need:

Felt in the colors you'd like to use

Scissors

Hot glue gun and hot glue sticks or a needle and strong thread

Cotton batting

Yarn or ribbon for the tail

Small jingle bells (optional)

Catnip (optional)

Step 1

Cut out page 29 from the book. Follow the dotted lines to cut out the pattern pieces.

Step 2

Use the pattern pieces to cut out shapes from the felt: two sides, a bottom, and ears.

Step 3

Glue or sew together the top edges of the side pieces.

Step 4

Glue or sew together the edges of the bottom piece to the side pieces. Leave an opening at the end.

Create your own felt mouse
TEMPLATE

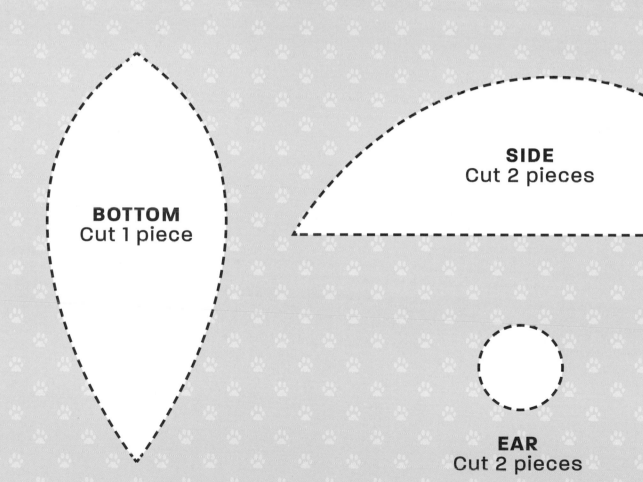

BOTTOM
Cut 1 piece

SIDE
Cut 2 pieces

EAR
Cut 2 pieces

Step 5

Add batting and, if desired, catnip and/or several bells to the inside of the mouse.

Step 6

Place the end of the yarn or ribbon inside the mouse and sew or glue the open edges closed.

Step 7

Sew or glue on the ears and, if desired, eyes and nose. The eyes and nose can also be drawn on with a marker.

'NIP KNOTS

What you'll need:

Scissors

A swath of clean cotton cloth

Catnip

Step 1

Cut a piece of fabric about 6 x 4 inches.

Step 2

Place a mound of catnip in the bottom center of the fabric.

Step 3

Working from the center, knot the fabric securely.

CATNIP FACTS

🐾 It's estimated that only about 60 to 70 percent of cats respond to catnip.

🐾 Baby kittens don't respond to catnip. They start to respond when they're a couple months old.

🐾 It's not just housecats that are affected! Many big cats like leopards, lynx, and tigers also love catnip!

🐾 You can keep catnip fresh and strong by storing it in the freezer in an airtight container.

Are these
my paws?!?

TO COSTUME OR NOT

There's some argument among cat owners over whether or not costumes are a good idea for cats. Some argue that they make cats unhappy and even scare them; others point to specific cats that will happily let you dress them for Halloween, Christmas, and every other occasion. If you do want to try costuming your cat, here are some tips:

 Let your cat become accustomed to the costume in the days before you want him to wear it. Leave the costume in the cat's area so that it will begin to take on the cat's scent.

 Make sure the costume is sturdy and doesn't have any parts, such as string, that can be torn off or swallowed.

🐾 Don't put on costumes that are tight or reduce the cat's range of vision or motion. Don't put on costumes that cover your cat's paws or face.

🐾 Young cats may respond better to costumes than older cats.

🐾 If your cat seems unhappy, take the costume off immediately.

I am *not* a hoppy bunny!

Teaching Your Cat
TRICKS

In a cat's eye,

all things belong to cats.

—English proverb

Can cats be trained? To some people—and perhaps to some cats—the mere idea of training a cat sounds like a joke. But while cats are by nature independent animals, with enough patience and the right reward, they can be taught to do almost anything.

For best results, practice right before your pet's mealtime. A hungry cat is a responsive cat.

One of the most important things to remember in training is to use a calm, gentle voice. Tricks should be taught in an area or in a room that is free of distractions so you and your pet can concentrate on the lesson being taught.

Above all, make sure the training is fun for you and your cat. Cats respond to rewards, not punishment. Keep your training sessions short. Don't expect to spend an hour on learning a trick. Instead, try to spend five or ten minutes a day, and practice each day. If at any point you feel yourself getting frustrated or angry, or if your cat is clearly losing interest, stop the training session.

Patience is key: You may need to spend more time and repetition than originally planned. But keep at it! Once your pet learns a new trick, you'll have a deeper appreciation for him, and he'll be happy to get your affection and a tasty reward.

CLICKERS

One of the best training tools you can invest in is a small handheld clicker that you can buy at any pet store. You can teach your cat to associate the clicking sound with a treat (food is the usual motivator, but it's not the only one). Each time the cat responds to the clicking sound, reward him with a small treat. Soon he will have a positive association with the sound. You can then click to reward those behaviors you want to encourage.

Use the clicker as soon as the cat does what you want. Keep the association between the behavior and the sound as strong as possible.

TOUCH AN OBJECT

One easy, impressive trick you can teach your cat is to touch a specific object on command. Get your handheld clicker and a small object, like a small rubber ball, and you'll be ready to go.

In a room free of distractions, place the object a few inches from your pet. Whenever she looks at or does anything in connection with the object, click the clicker and reward her with a treat.

Practice at the same time every day, clicking and rewarding each time your cat approaches or touches the object.

After a while, she will realize that pawing the object means food, and she'll begin touching it with the intended purpose of receiving a reward. Start giving the command "Touch the object." Say this the moment before you click as your pet reaches for the object.

With sufficient practice, your pet will automatically touch the object upon your command. You don't have to click and reward every time she performs this trick, but you should do so most of the time to reinforce the desired behavior. If you don't, your pet will grow bored and stop responding to your command.

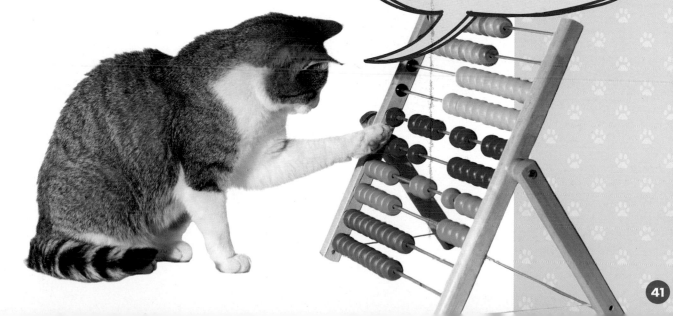

By the end of the week they should owe me... 26 treats.

SIT

In a quiet room, stand in front of your cat with a treat in your hand. Show her the treat so she is aware of it. Raise your hand up and over her head toward her back just a little bit; as she follows your hand with her head, her body will automatically fall into a sitting position. The moment she does this, reward her with the treat and give her some praise.

Once your cat becomes used to sitting by following your hand, start using the "Sit" command.

Say this right before she sits, then reward her with a treat. Practice for 10 minutes a day, every day, until she begins sitting on command. You don't have to reward her every time, but you should do so often enough to reinforce the behavior.

You can also use a handheld clicker as part of the training. Click right before your cat sits and receives a reward as a form of positive reinforcement.

All cats can learn this trick, but younger cats tend to pick it up a little more quickly than older cats who are more set in their ways.

If your cat reaches up or jumps for the snack in your hand, you are holding it too far above our head. Four to six inches is a good distance.

Did I hear the treat container ...? I mean, did you call me?

COME WHEN CALLED

Teaching your cat to come on command serves two functions: It guarantees feline companionship whenever you want it, and it also ensures your pet's safety during an emergency by making your cat easy to locate.

Cats are extremely intelligent animals and can be taught to do almost anything. However, they need the right motivation. Some cats will come when you call simply because they like to be petted, but others may need more incentive—such as a yummy snack or treat.

To make this trick work, you should start training your cat when he is young. Call him by name every time you play together, and reward him with affection whenever he approaches you.

Before long, he should respond positively every time you call him. If, however, your cat still refuses to come despite your affection, it may be time to try a different approach. Continue to say his name every time you play, but now reward him with a snack when he comes to you. Soon your cat will associate his name with a treat and come on command, a phenomenon known as the Pavlovian response.

Once the behavior is firmly established, gradually substitute praise for food. To keep him motivated, however, you should still occasionally reward him with a treat.

Keep in mind that kindness goes a long way when training a cat. Never be too forceful or yell in anger or frustration. This will only frighten your cat and make the teaching process more difficult.

EAT ON CUE

Dog owners commonly train their pets to wait for a signal before eating their food. In fact, a very well-trained dog will even wait for the right cue before consuming a treat placed on his nose! Cats can also be trained to wait for a signal before eating something, but don't attempt the nose trick; no self-respecting feline will let you go that far!

In a room free of distractions, sit on the floor with your cat in front of you. Place a treat between you and your pet, and hold your hand over it while giving the "Wait" command. Raise your hand. If your cat tries to eat the snack, use your hand to gently block her. Repeat the "Wait" command as you do this. Continue this exercise until your cat waits a few seconds as instructed, then give the "Go" command and allow her to eat the treat.

As training progresses, give the "Go" command at the instant your pet reaches for the treat.

With enough practice, she will hold steady at the "Wait" command and won't reach for her treat until she hears you say "Go." Of course, this is counterintuitive to a cat's natural instincts, so don't give up if your pet doesn't grasp the concept right away. Practice makes perfect.

Hint: If your cat insists on going for the treat despite your best attempts to get her to wait, remove the treat, let her calm down, then try again.

LIE DOWN

Once your cat has learned to sit, teaching him to lie down is not too much of a stretch.

When your cat is in a sitting position, hold a treat in front of his nose and lower it to the floor. He will likely follow it down, finally resting on his stomach.

Once he is on his stomach, give him the treat and praise him.

After practicing this a few times, start the trick by saying your cat's name along with the command, "Down."

Hint: If the treat in your hand isn't enough to coax your cat down, try gently nudging his shoulder blades to help him along.

The easy method:

Wait for your cat to lie down. Whisper "good cat" and pretend you had something to do with his choice.

ROLL OVER

Your cat can learn this trick in two parts. To begin, make sure your cat is in the "Down" position. Kneel beside her, take a treat, and put it in front of her nose. Say "Roll over," and move the treat toward your cat's shoulder blade in the direction you'd like her to roll. Once she has rolled onto her side, reward her with a treat.

When your cat is used to rolling onto her side, It's time to take her the rest of the way. Instead of rewarding her after just a side roll, move the treat from her shoulder blade toward her spine so she will follow it and roll over the rest of the way. Once your cat has touched her other side to the floor, reward her with the treat.

It's easier if you try to teach this trick on a carpet or other soft surface. We may be uncomfortable rolling over if the surface is too hard.

SHAKE HANDS

Cats tend to come in two types: aloof and extremely affectionate. But regardless of your pet's temperament, she should have little trouble learning how to shake hands. All it takes is a little practice and the right incentive.

With your cat sitting in front of you, hold a treat in one hand and touch one paw with your other hand. When she raises the paw, hold it gently while saying "Shake." Reward your pet with the treat and say "Good girl!" Repeat two or three more times, always with the proper command and a treat after a successful shake.

Aw yeah, I got this down now! Give me some paw!

With enough practice, your cat should start raising her paw on her own in anticipation of a treat. When she does, give her your palm for a furry high-five.

Cats learn best through repetition, so try to practice this trick at the same time every day. (Right before mealtime works well because your cat will be more responsive to a food reward.) Keep the training brief, and stop at the first sign that your pet is losing interest.

Hint: Get your cat's attention by saying her name while giving the "Shake" command.

Are you sure about this?!? I'm not!

WALK ON A HARNESS AND LEASH

Not all cats adapt well to wearing a leash, but some love the chance to put one on and explore the great outdoors!

The first step is to buy an adjustable harness and leash. (Don't opt for a collar—even cats that aren't normally escape artists might slip through one.) Let the cat explore the harness, sniffing it and determining that it is safe, before you attempt to put it on for the first time. You may even want to leave the harness and leash in the cat's area for several days, so that the scent and sight of it will become familiar.

When you put the harness on for the first time, do so at a mealtime, and reward the cat with a treat. Make sure that the harness fits comfortably and doesn't impede your cat's movements. Over the course of several days, let your cat become accustomed to wearing the harness by itself for short periods around the house. Praise the cat and reward her with treats and attention each time she does so.

Follow me!

When your cat is accustomed to the harness, attach the leash. Again, let your cat become accustomed to wearing the leash around the house. However, do keep a close eye on your cat during these times—you don't want the leash to get tangled around something. When your cat is comfortable with the leash, take up the other end. At first, follow your cat where she leads. Then begin to direct the walk. You can use treats to guide the cat in the direction you want to go. Take care that it doesn't become a battle of wills.

When you do take your cat outside, take your cat to a quiet area—a fenced-in backyard is ideal.

Hint: If your cat seems reluctant at any stage, go back to the previous stage, and let your cat set the pace for moving to the next one.

> Caution: Before you teach your cat this trick, consider carefully. Do you want your cat to have power over light and darkness?

TURN THE LIGHTS OFF

Teaching your cat to turn off the lights is a simple trick that is both entertaining and useful. Begin by holding the feathered cat training toy (see page 24) or your cat's favorite treat against the wall a few inches above the light switch. (A traditional flip switch works best.) Give the order "Lights" and reward your pet with the treat when he successfully scratches at the switch. Repeat as necessary.

Next, enhance this behavior by holding a treat in your hand above the switch and a few inches away from the wall. Tap the switch with your free hand while repeating the order "Lights." Praise him, and release the treat when he rises upright or jumps up and paws the wall two or three times. Once your cat gets the idea, tap the light switch while giving the order "Lights," then lower your hands and let your pet paw the wall by himself. Reward him every time he successfully paws the switch and turns the lights off. Repeat this exercise until your cat has it figured out.

For the final step, stand across the room and give the order "Lights." Your cat should rise up or jump up and paw at the switch as instructed. Reward him with affection and a treat every time he is successful. Before you know it, your cat will be turning the lights off on command.

If your cat can flip a light switch, he might even be able to turn a door handle. Watch out, world!

FETCH

This trick uses two small balls to get things started. Hold one ball where it can get your cat's attention. Once your cat is interested, toss the ball a few feet away and say, "Fetch."

If your cat gets the ball but doesn't bring it back, use the "Come" command. However, even if she returns, she may not want to give you the ball, which is where the second ball comes in. Present the second ball to her, maybe tossing it from hand to hand or tossing it up and down in one hand—whatever you can do to make it appealing to her. When she drops the first ball and allows you to pick it up, give her a treat, and toss the second ball for her to retrieve.

Although you need to repeat the trick and practice, make sure that you don't practice so long that your cat gets bored by the activity.

You can play fetch with any toy your cat likes, or even something as simple as a ball of paper.

Hint: Different breeds have different levels of interest in fetching. Young cats may be particularly interested in and successful with this trick.

I was worshiped by the Egyptians. So, no, humans bring me things, not the other way around.

JUMP THROUGH A HOOP

Jumping through a hoop is a classic trick, and one of the easiest things to teach your pet.

Begin by purchasing a hula hoop or similar toy if you don't already have one. (If the hoop comes with beads inside, remove them; the noise can be frightening or distracting.) Hold the hoop vertically on the floor with one hand, then give the command "Hoop" and lure your cat through the hoop with a treat or by dangling the feathered cat training toy (see page 24) on the other side. If your pet continually tries to go around the hoop instead of through it, position the hoop in a doorway to block his way.

Repeat this a few times until your cat easily walks through the hoop on command. Once he's comfortable, raise the hoop a few inches off the ground and repeat, again using a treat as a reward. Over the course of a few days, gradually raise the hoop higher and higher until your cat must jump to get through it. Many cats are great jumpers and won't need much encouragement!

Practice until your pet enthusiastically leaps through the hoop on your command.

If your cat trips while going through the hoop, release it immediately to avoid injury. Continue training as if nothing happened; if you react negatively to such an incident, your pet may pick up on your emotions and become afraid of the hoop.

Make this trick more exciting by decorating the hoop with colored ribbons and other dazzlers. Make sure they don't distract your cat or get in his way.

RUN AN OBSTACLE COURSE

It's easier than you might think to turn your cat into a four-footed Olympian by teaching her how to run an obstacle course. Not only will she have fun, but running a course is also great exercise.

Create a small course in your living room using household objects such as cardboard boxes, plastic tubs, stacked books, wood planks (detachable bookshelves work well), chairs, and pillows. If you're good with your hands, you can also construct platforms on poles, or purchase them premade at any pet supply store.

Give your cat a day or two to explore the various items that make up the course, then begin training. After you have your cat's attention, stand in the middle of the course and drag the feathered cat training toy found in this kit (see page 24) or another favorite cat toy tied to a string along the various obstacles. Your cat will chase the toy over, through, and across everything in her path in an attempt to catch it. At the end of the course, reward your pet with a treat.

Practice two or three times a day, stopping when your cat begins to lose interest. Once she becomes adept at running the course, put on a show for family and friends.

Hint: Don't expect your cat to run the course without your participation. Unlike other tricks, this one is usually dependent on giving her something to chase.

*What greater gift
than the love of a cat?*

—Charles Dickens